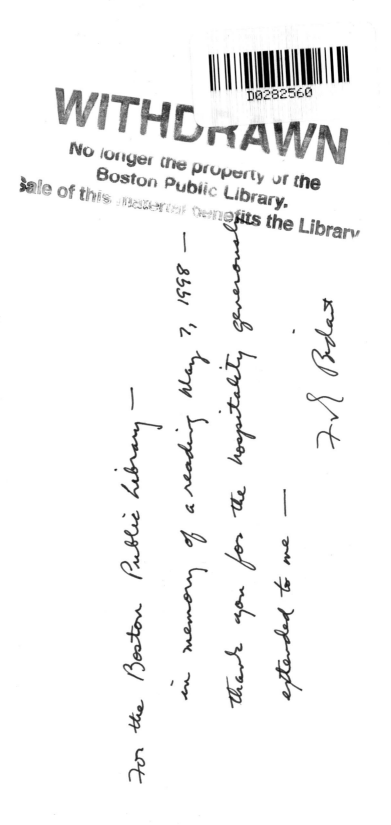

For the Boston Public library —

in memory of a reading May 7, 1998 —

thank you for the hospitality generously

extended to me —

F.D. Reeve

DESIRE

DESIRE

FRANK
BIDART

Farrar, Straus and Giroux

New York

Farrar, Straus and Giroux
19 Union Square West, New York 10003

Copyright © 1997 by Frank Bidart
All rights reserved
Distributed in Canada by Douglas & McIntyre Ltd.
Printed in the United States of America
First edition, 1997
Second printing, 1997

*The poems in this volume first appeared in the following
publications:* Antaeus, Electronic Poetry Review, Harvard
Review, Lingo, The New Yorker, The Paris Review, The
Threepenny Review, *and* Who's Writing This? *(The Ecco Press,
1995).*

Library of Congress Cataloging-in-Publication Data
Bidart, Frank, 1939–
    Desire / Frank Bidart.
      p.   cm.
    Poetry.
    ISBN 0-374-13824-9 (cloth : alk. paper)
    I. Title.
    PS3552.I33D47   1997
    811'.54—dc21   97-9098

Contents

I

AS THE EYE TO THE SUN

To Plotinus what we seek is VISION, what
wakes when we wake to desire

as the eye to the sun

It is just as if you should fall in love with
one of the sparrows which fly by

when we wake to desire

But once you have seen a hand cut off, or
a foot, or a head, you have embarked, have begun

as the eye to the sun

The voyage, such is everything, you have not come to
shore, but little children and their sports and

when we wake to desire

Poor spirits carrying about bodies of the dead,
for bodies give way but the spirit will not give way

as the eye to the sun

You know that every instrument, too, vessel, mere
hammer, if it does that for which it was made

when we wake to desire

Is well, yet he who made it is not there, is dead:
so, unaverted, one, not one, to NOTHING you ask

as the eye to the sun

May I be made into the vessel of that which
must be made

when we wake to desire

Certain what you have reached is not shore you
shall disappear in that which produced you

as the eye to the sun

But once you have seen a hand cut off you have begun

LOVE INCARNATE

(Dante, *Vita Nuova*)

To all those driven berserk or humanized by love
this is offered, for I need help
deciphering my dream.
When we love our lord is LOVE.

When I recall that at the fourth hour
of the night, watched by shining stars,
LOVE at last became incarnate,
the memory is horror.

In his hands smiling LOVE held my burning
heart, and in his arms, the body whose greeting
pierces my soul, now wrapped in bloodred, sleeping.

He made him wake. He ordered him to eat
my heart. He ate my burning heart. He ate it
submissively, as if afraid, as LOVE wept.

OVERHEARD THROUGH THE WALLS

OF THE INVISIBLE CITY

. . . telling those who swarm around him his desire
is that an appendage from each of them
fill, invade each of his orifices, —

repeating, chanting,
Oh yeah   Oh yeah   Oh yeah   Oh yeah   Oh yeah

until, as if in darkness he craved the sun, at last he reached
consummation.

—Until telling those who swarm around him begins again

(we are the wheel to which we are bound).

ADOLESCENCE

He stared up into my eyes with a look
I can almost see now.

He had that look in his eyes
that bore right into mine.

I could sense that he *knew* I was
envious of what he was doing—; and *knew* that I'd

always wish I had known at the time
what he was doing was something I'd always

crave in later life, just as he did.

He was enjoying what he was doing.
The look was one of pure rapture.

He was gloating. He knew.

I still remember his look.

Catullus: Excrucior

I hate and—love. The sleepless body hammering a nail nails itself, hanging crucified.

We fill pre-existing forms and when we fill them we change them and are changed.

The desolating landscape in Borges' "Borges and I"—in which the voice of "I" tells us that its other self, Borges, is the self who makes literature, who in the process of making literature falsifies and exaggerates, while the self that is speaking to us now must go on living so that Borges may continue to fashion literature—is seductive and even oddly comforting, but, I think, false.

The voice of this "I" asserts a disparity between its essential self and its worldly second self, the self who seeks embodiment through making things, through work, who in making takes on something false, inessential, inauthentic.

The voice of this "I" tells us that Spinoza understood that everything wishes to continue in its own being, a stone wishes to be a stone eternally, that all "I" wishes is to remain unchanged, itself.

With its lonely emblematic title, "Borges and I" seems to be offered as a paradigm for the life of consciousness, the life of knowing and making, the life of the writer.

The notion that Frank has a self that has remained the same and that knows what it would be if its writing self did not exist—like all assertions about the systems that hold sway beneath the moon, the opposite of this seems to me to be true, as true.

When Borges' "I" confesses that Borges falsifies and exaggerates it seems to do so to cast aside falsity and exaggeration, to attain an entire candor unobtainable by Borges.

This "I" therefore allows us to enter an inaccessible magic space, a hitherto inarticulate space of intimacy and honesty earlier denied us, where voice, for the first time, has replaced silence.

—Sweet fiction, in which bravado and despair beckon from a cold panache, in which the protected essential self suffers flashes of its existence to be immortalized by a writing self that is incapable of performing its actions without mixing our essence with what is false.

Frank had the illusion, when he talked to himself in the cliches he used when he talked to himself, that when he made his poems he was changed in making them, that arriving at the order the poem suddenly arrived at out of the chaos of the materials the poem let enter itself out of the chaos of life, consciousness then, only then, could know itself, Sherlock Holmes was somebody or something before cracking its first case but not Sherlock Holmes, act is the cracked mirror not only of motive but self, *no other way*, tiny mirror that fails to focus in small the whole of the great room.

But Frank had the illusion that his poems also had cruelly replaced his past, that finally they were all he knew of it though he knew they were not, everything else was shards refusing to make a pattern and in any case he had written about his mother and father until the poems saw as much as he saw and saw more and he only saw what he saw in the act of making them.

He had never had a self that wished to continue in its own being, survival meant ceasing to be what its being was.

Frank had the illusion that though the universe of one of his poems seemed so close to what seemed his own universe at the second of writing it that he wasn't sure how they differed even though the paraphernalia often differed, after he had written it its universe was never exactly his universe, and so, soon, it disgusted him a little, the mirror was dirty and cracked.

Secretly he was glad it was dirty and cracked, because after he had made a big order, a book, only when he had come to despise it a little, only after he had at last given up the illusion that this was what was, only then could he write more.

He felt terror at the prospect of becoming again the person who could find or see or make no mirror, for even Olivier, trying to trap the beast who had killed his father, when he suavely told Frank as Frank listened to the phonograph long afternoons lying on the bed as a kid, when Olivier told him what art must be, even Olivier insisted that art is a mirror held up by an artist who himself needs to see something, held up before a nature that recoils before it.

We fill pre-existing forms and when we fill them we change them and are changed.

Everything in art is a formal question, so he tried to do it in prose with much blank white space.

HOMO FABER

Whatever lies still uncarried from the abyss within
me as I die dies with me.

IN MEMORY OF JOE BRAINARD

the remnant of a vast, oceanic
bruise (wound delivered early and long ago)

was in you purity and
sweetness self-gathered, CHOSEN

•

When I tried to find words for the moral sense that unifies
and sweetens the country voices in your collage *The Friendly Way,*

you said *It's a code.*

You were a code
I yearned to decipher.—

In the end, the plague that full swift runs by
took you, broke you;—

> *in the end, could not*
> *take you, did not break you—*

you had somehow erased within you not only
meanness, but anger, the desire to punish
the universe for everything

not achieved, *not* tasted, seen again, touched—;

. . . the undecipherable
code unbroken even as the soul

learns once again the body it loves and hates is
made of earth, and will betray it.

THE YOKE

don't worry   I know you're dead
but tonight

turn your face again
toward me

when I hear your voice there is now
no direction in which to turn

I sleep and wake and sleep and wake and sleep and wake and

but tonight
turn your face again

toward me

see   upon my shoulders is the yoke
that is not a yoke

don't worry   I know you're dead
but tonight

turn your face again

LADY BIRD

Neither an invalid aunt who had been asked to care for a sister's
little girl, to fill the dead sister's place, nor the child herself

did, could: not in my Daddy's eyes—nor
should they;

                so when we followed that golden couple into the White House

I was aware that people look at
the living, and wish for the dead.

IF I COULD MOURN LIKE A MOURNING DOVE

It is what recurs that we believe,
your face not at one moment looking
sideways up at me anguished or

elate, but the old words welling up by
gravity rearranged:
two weeks before you died in

pain worn out, after my usual casual sign-off
with *All my love*, your simple
solemn *My love to you, Frank*.

THE RETURN

As the retreating Bructeri began to burn their own
possessions, to deny to the Romans every sustenance but
ashes,

      a flying column sent by Germanicus
commanded by Lucius Stertinius

routed them;
         and there, discovered amid plunder and the dead,

was the Eagle of the nineteenth
legion, lost with Varus.

      •

The Romans now
brought to the land of the Bructeri,—to whatever lay
between the river Ems and the river Lippe,
to the very edge of their territory,—
         devastation;

until they reached at last

the Teutoburgian Wood,
        in whose darkness

Varus and the remains of his fifteen thousand men,
it was said, lay unburied.

      •

Germanicus then conceived a desire
to honor with obsequies these unburied warriors whose

massacre once filled Augustus himself with rage and
shame,—
        with hope or fear every corner of the Empire,—

while the least foot soldier, facing alien
terrain, was overcome with pity when he

thought of family, friends, the sudden
reversals of battle, and shared human fate.

        •

First Caecina and his men
entered,—
        ordered to reconnoitre the dismal

treacherous passes, to attempt to build bridges and
causeways across the uneven, sodden marshland,—

then the rest of the army, witness to scenes
rending to sight and memory of sight.

        •

Varus' first camp, with its wide sweep and deployment
of ordered space in confident dimension,
testified to the calm labors of three legions;—

then a ruined half-wall and shallow ditch
showed where a desperate remnant had
been driven to take cover;—

        on the open ground between them

were whitening bones, free
from putrefaction,—

scattered where men had been struck down
fleeing, heaped up

where they had stood their ground before slaughter.

Fragments of spears and horses' limbs lay
intertwined, while human

                    skulls were nailed

like insults to the tree-trunks.

Nearby groves held the altars
on which the savage Germans
sacrificed the tribunes and chief centurions.

         •

Survivors of the catastrophe slowly began, at last,
to speak,—
         the handful who had escaped death or slavery

told their fellow soldiers where the generals
fell, how the Eagles and standards were seized;—

one showed where Varus received his first wound, and
another, where he died by his own melancholy hand;—

those thrown into crude pits saw
gibbets above them,
         as well as the platform from which Arminius

as if in delirium harangued
his own victorious troops,—

fury and rancor so joined to his
joy, the imprisoned men thought they would soon be butchered,—

until desecration of the Eagles at last satisfied
or exhausted his arrogance.

                  •

And so, six years after the slaughter,
a living Roman army had returned
to bury the dead men's bones of three whole legions,—

no man knew whether the remains that he had
gathered, touched perhaps in consigning to the earth, were

those of a stranger or a friend:—
                          all thought of all
as comrades and
bloodbrothers; each, in common rising

fury against the enemy, mourned at once and hated.

                  •

When these events were reported to Rome

Cynics whispered that *thus* the cunning State
enslaves us to its failures and its fate.—

Epicureans saw in the ghostly mire
an emblem of the nature of Desire.—

Stoics replied that life is War, ILLUSION
the source, the goal, the end of human action.

                  •

At the dedication of the funeral
mound, Germanicus laid the first earth,—

thereby honoring the dead, and choosing to demonstrate
in his own person his
heartfelt share in the general grief.

He thereby earned the disapproval of Tiberius,—

perhaps because the Emperor interpreted
every action of Germanicus unfavorably; or he may have felt

the spectacle of the unburied dead
must give the army less alacrity for battle and more
respect for the enemy—
                    while a commander belonging to

the antique priesthood of the Augurs
pollutes himself by handling
objects belonging to the dead.

                •

            on the open ground

*whitening bones scattered where men had been struck down
fleeing*

        heaped up

where they stood their ground

*Varus' first camp with its
wide sweep*

            across the open ground

*the ruined
half-wall and shallow ditch*

                on the open ground between them

whitening bones scattered where men had been struck down
fleeing

      heaped up

where they stood their ground

I have returned here a thousand times,
though history cannot tell us its location.

      •

Arminius, relentlessly pursued by
Germanicus, retreated into pathless country.

      (After Tacitus, *Annals*, I, 60–63)

A COIN FOR JOE, WITH THE IMAGE
OF A HORSE; C. 350–325 BC

COIN

chip of the closed,—L O S T world, toward whose unseen grasses

this long-necked emissary horse

> *eagerly still*
> *stretches, to graze*

.

World; Grass;

stretching Horse;—ripe with hunger, bright circle
of appetite, risen to feed and famish us, from exile underground . . . for

you   chip of the incommensurate
closed world   *A n g e l*

II

THE SECOND HOUR OF THE NIGHT

On such a night

       after the countless

assemblies, countless solemnities, the infinitely varied
voyagings in storm and in calm observing the differences

among those who are born, who live together, and die,

     •

On such a night

      at that hour when

slow bodies like automatons begin again to move down

into the earth beneath the houses in which they
live bearing the bodies they desired and killed and now

bury in the narrow crawl spaces and unbreathing abrupt
descents and stacked leveled spaces these used

bodies make them dig and open out and hollow for new
veins whose ore could have said *I have been loved* but whose

voice has been rendered silent by the slow bodies whose descent
into earth is as fixed as the skeletons buried within them

     •

On such a night

        at that hour in the temple of

delight, when appetite
feeds on itself,—

       •

On such a night, perhaps, Berlioz wrote those pages

in his autobiography which I first read when my mother
was dying, and which to me now inextricably
call up

      not only her death but her life:—

"A sheet already covered her. I drew it back.

Her portrait, painted in the days of
her splendor,

      hung beside the bed—

I will not attempt to describe the grief that possessed me.

It was complicated by something, *incommensurate,*
tormenting, I had always found hardest to bear—

a sense of pity.

      Terrible, overmastering

pity swept through me at everything she had suffered:—

Before our marriage,
her bankruptcy.

(Dazed, almost
appalled by the magnitude of her sudden
and early Paris triumph—as Ophelia, as Juliet—
she risked the fortune fame had brought
on the fidelity of a public without memory.)

Her accident.

(Just before a benefit
performance designed to lessen, if not
erase her debts, a broken leg left her
NOT—as the doctors feared—lame, but visibly
robbed of confidence and ease of movement.)

Her humiliating
return to the Paris stage.

(After Ophelia's
death, which a few years earlier at her debut
harrowed the heart of Paris, the cruel
audience did not recall her to the stage
once, though it accorded others an ovation.)

Her decision, made voluntarily but forever
mourned, to give up her art.

Extinction of her reputation.

The wounds each of us
inflicted on the other.

Her not-to-be-extinguished, insane JEALOUSY,—
. . . which, in the end, had cause.

Our separation, after eleven years.

The enforced
absence of our son.

Her delusion that she had forfeited the regard of
the English public, through her attachment to France.

Her broken heart.

Her vanished beauty.

Her ruined health. (Corrosive, and growing,
physical pain.)

The loss of speech,—
. . . and movement.

The impossibility of making herself understood in any way.

The long vista of death and oblivion stretching before her
as she lay paralyzed for four years, inexorably dying.

—My brain shrivels in my skull
at the horror, the PITY of it.

Her simple tomb bears the inscription:

> *Henriette-Constance Berlioz-Smithson, born at*
> *Ennis in Ireland, died at Montmartre 3rd March 1854*

At eight in the evening the day of her death
as I struggled across Paris to notify
the Protestant minister required for the ceremony,

the cab in which I rode, *vehicle*
conceived in Hell, made a detour and

took me past the Odeon:—

it was brightly lit for a play then much in vogue.

There, twenty-six years before, I discovered
Shakespeare and Miss Smithson at the same moment.

Hamlet. Ophelia. There
I saw Juliet for the first and last time.

Within the darkness of that arcade on many
winter nights I feverishly
paced or watched frozen in despair.

Through that door I saw her enter
for a rehearsal of *Othello*.

She was unaware of the existence of
the pale dishevelled youth with
haunted eyes staring after her—

There I asked the gods to allow her
future to rest in my hands.

If anyone should ask you, Ophelia, whether the unknown
youth without reputation or position
leaning back within the darkness of a pillar

will one day become your
husband and prepare your last journey—

with your great inspired eyes

answer, *He is a harbinger of woe."*

•

On such a night, at such an hour

she who still carries within her body the growing
body made by union with what she once loved, and now

31

craves or
loathes, she cannot say—;

she who has seen the world and her own self and the gods

within the mirror of
Dionysus, as it were—

compelled to labor since birth in care of the care-
needing thing into which she had entered;—

. . . Myrrha, consigning now to

the body heavier and heavier within her
what earlier she could consign only to air,

requests

in death transformation to nothing
human, to be not alive, not dead.

I I

Ovid tells the tale:—
                    or, rather, Ovid tells us that

Orpheus sang it
in that litany of tales with which he

filled the cruel silence after Eurydice
had been sucked back down into the underworld
cruelly and he driven back cruelly
from descending into it again to save her . . .

He sang it on a wide green plain
without shade,
                    but there the trees, as if
mimicking the attending beasts and birds, hearing his song

came to listen: the alder, the yew, the laurel
and pine whose young sweet nut
is dear to the mother of the gods since under it
Attis castrated himself to become her votary and vessel . . .

Beasts; birds; trees; but by his will
empty of gods or men.

                    •

In each tale of love he sang,—
                    Ganymede; Apollo and
Hyacinthus; Pygmalion; Adonis avenged upon
Venus; the apples that Atalanta found irresistible,—

fate embedded in the lineaments of desire

(desire itself helplessly surrounded by what cannot be
eluded, what
even the gods call GIVEN,—)

at last, in bitter or sweet enforcement, finds

transformation (except for the statue
Pygmalion makes human) to an inhuman, un-
riven state, become an element, indelible,
common, in the common, indelible, given world . . .

The story of Myrrha, mother of Adonis, is of all
these tales for good reason the least known.

It is said that Cinyras, her father, had he been
childless, might have died a happy man.

Famed both for his gold and for his beauty, Cinyras
had become King of Cyprus and of Byblus

by marrying the daughter of the king, Myrrha's
mother, whose father had become king by marrying the daughter

of the king, Myrrha's mother's
mother, Paphos,—

. . . *child*
born from the union of Pygmalion and the statue.

When the eyes of Cinyras
followed, lingered upon her, Myrrha had the sensation
he was asking himself whether, in
another world, she could heal him.

Myrrha was Pygmalion and her father the statue.

He was Pygmalion and Myrrha the statue.

—As a dog whose body is sinking into quicksand
locks its jaws around a branch hanging
above it, the great teeth grasping so fiercely the stable world
they snap the fragile wood,—

. . . Myrrha looped a rope over the beam above her bed

in order to hang herself.

What she wants she does not want.

The night she could no longer NOT tell herself
her secret, she knew that there had never
been a time she had not known it.

It was there like the island

that, night after
night, as she

wished herself to sleep, she embellished
the approach to:—

the story has many beginnings, but one ending—

out of the air she has invented it, air
she did not invent . . .

.

In the earliest version whose making and remaking Myrrha
remembers,
    she and her father escape from Cyprus

in a small boat, swallowed, protected
by a storm that blackens sea and stars;

he has been stripped of power by advisors of the dead
old king, father of Myrrha's mother, Queen
Cenchreis, and now, the betrayers make Cenchreis

head of state,—

Cinyras in the storm shouts that they have made his
wife their pawn, and Myrrha shouts that many
long have thought
     they are HERS,—

. . . the storm, after days,
abandons them to face a chartless, terrifying horizon.

Then, the island.

In the version that Myrrha now
tells herself since both her father and mother as
King and Queen insist that with their concurrence

soon, from among the royal
younger sons who daily arrive at court as rivals for
her bed, she must choose a husband—

both for her own natural happiness, and
to secure the succession,—

. . . now she is too violated by the demand that she marry

to invent reasons why the story that she
tells herself to calm herself to sleep begins with
a powerless king standing next to his
daughter in a tiny boat as they stare out at
a distant, yearned-for, dreaded island . . .

On the island, later, she again and again relives
stepping onto the island.

Each of them knows what will happen here:—

. . . she can delay, he can delay
because what is sweet about
deferral is that what arrives

despite it, is revealed as inevitable:—

she is awake
only during the lucid
instant between what she recognizes

must happen, and what happens:—

each of them knows that the coldest eye looking
down at them, here, must look without blame:—

now, the king
hesitates—

       he refuses to place his foot upon the shore:—

. . . the illusion of rescue from what he is, what
she is, soon must recede, once on
land everything
not nature fall away,

            as unstarved springs

divide them from all that
divide them from themselves:—

*bulls fuck cows they
sired, Zeus himself fathered Dionysus-Zagreus
upon Persephone, his daughter:—*

beasts and gods, those
below us and those above us, open
unhuman eyes

when they gaze upon what they desire
unstained by disgust or dread or terror:—

. . . Myrrha, watching him, now once again can close her eyes
upon sleep. She sees him

step onto the island. He has entered her.

           •

Grief for the unlived life, grief
which, in middle age or old age, as goad

or shroud, comes to all,

early became Myrrha's
familiar, her narcotic

chastisement, accomplice, master.

What each night she had given with such
extravagance,—

. . . when she woke, had not been given.

Grief for the unlived life, mourning
each morning renewed as Myrrha

woke, was there

and not there, for hours merely
the memory of itself, as if long ago

she told herself
a story *(weird*

dream of enslavement) that seemed
her story, but now she cannot

recollect why listening she could not
stop listening, deaf to any other . . .

But soon she heard the music beneath every other music:—

what she could not transform herself
into is someone

without memory, or need for memory:—

four steps forward then
one back, then three
back, then four forward . . .

Today when Myrrha's father reminded her that
on this date eighteen
years earlier her mother announced that he
was the man whom she would in one month

marry,—

and then, in exasperation, asked what Myrrha
wanted in a husband, unsupplied by the young men cluttering his
court in pursuit of her hand and his throne,—

after she, smiling, replied, "You,"

blushing, he turned
away, pleased . . .

Four steps forward then
one back, then three
back, then four forward:—

today her father, not ten feet from where
once, as a child, she had in
glee leapt upon him surrounded by
soldiers and he, then, pretending to be overwhelmed
by a superior force fell backwards with
her body clasped in his arms as they rolled
body over body down the long slope
laughing and that peculiar sensation of his weight
full upon her and then
not, then full upon her, then not,—

until at the bottom for a half-
second his full weight rested upon her, then not,—

. . . not ten feet from where what
never had been repeated except within
her today after reminding her that today her mother

exactly at her age chose him,—

after she had answered his question
with, "You,"

blushing, he turned
away, pleased . . .

There is a king inside the king that the king
does not acknowledge.

Four steps forward then
one back, then three
back, then four forward:—

. . . the illusion of movement without
movement, because you know that what you
move towards

(malignant in the eyes of gods and men)

isn't there:—

        doesn't exist:—

though the sensation of motion without
movement or end offers the hypnotic

solace of making not only each repeated
act but what cannot be repeated

an object of contemplation,—

. . . what by rumor servant girls, and slaves, as well as
a foreign queen

        taste, for Myrrha alone

isn't there, doesn't exist,
malignant in the eyes of gods and men . . .

The gods who made us either
didn't make us,—

. . . or loathe what they have made.

Four steps forward then
one back, then three
back, then four forward:—

. . . but you have lied about your
solace, for hidden, threaded

within repetition is the moment when each step
backward is a step
downward, when what you move toward moves toward

you lifting painfully his cloak to reveal his
wound, saying, *"love answers need"* . . .

Approaching death, for days Myrrha more and more
talked to the air:—

My element is the sea. I have seen

the underside of the surface of the sea, the glittering
inner surface more beautiful than the darkness below it,

seen it crossed

and re-crossed by a glittering ship from which dark eyes
peering downward must search the darkness.

Though they search, the eyes
fix upon nothing.

The glittering ship swiftly,
evenly, crosses and re-crosses.

No hand reaches down from it to penetrate the final
membrane dividing those whose element
is the sea, from those who breathe in the light above it.

The glittering ship captained by darkness
swiftly, evenly, crosses and

re-crosses.

I have seen it. I cannot
forget. Memory is a fact of the soul.

·

Hippolyta, Myrrha's nurse, thanked the gods
she heard the thump of the rope

hitting the wooden beam, the scrape of
the heavy stool moved into place,

and clasped Myrrha's legs
just as they kicked away the light that held them.

—The creature plummeting resistlessly to the sunless
bottom of the sea was
plucked up, and placed upon the shore.

She slept. After a period of indefinite
duration Hippolyta's voice almost uninflected

woke her, saying that now her nurse must
know the reason for her action.

Failure had made her Hippolyta's
prisoner—; she

told her . . .

Head bowed deferentially, Hippolyta
listened without moving.

Hippolyta gathered up the rope, then
disappeared.

Myrrha slept. After a period of indefinite
duration Hippolyta's voice almost uninflected

woke her, saying that she had seen the King and
told the King that she could bring to him tonight a young

girl in love with him who wished to share
his bed, but who must, out of modesty, remain veiled.

Tonight the Festival of Demeter began, during
which the married women of Cyprus in
thanksgiving for the harvest, garlanded
with unthreshed
ears of wheat, robed in white, in secret
purification within the temple for nine days and
nights, abstained from their husbands' now-outlawed beds.

(Each year, Queen Cenchreis fulfilled with ostentatious
ardor the letter of the law.)

Hippolyta told Myrrha that when she
asked the King whether the King will

accept the girl, he asked
her age.

Hippolyta replied, "Myrrha's age."

The King then said, "*Yes.*"

Listening to Hippolyta's words Myrrha
knew that tonight she would allow Hippolyta in
darkness to lead her veiled to her father's chamber.

The door that did not exist

stood open—; she would
step through.

Hippolyta once again
disappeared.

                •

In her own room at last Hippolyta fell upon
her knees before her altar to the Furies.

Ten years earlier, when Menelaus and Odysseus
and Agamemnon's herald Talthybius
arrived in Cyprus seeking from the newly-crowned King
(Queen Cenchreis still wore mourning)

help for their expedition to humble Troy,—

. . . Cinyras, giddy not only with unfamiliar
obeisance to his power by men of power, but too much

wine, promised in six months to send sixty ships.

As a gift for Agamemnon, he gave his herald the breastplate
of the still-mourned King, gorgeously
worked with circles of cobalt and gold and tin, with two
serpents of cobalt rearing toward the neck.

Hippolyta and Myrrha overheard the Queen
next morning calmly tell the King that the great families who
chose the King's advisors had no intention of
honoring his drunken
grandiloquent bravado by funding sixty ships—

that if he persisted either the house of her
father must fall, or she would be forced
to renounce him and marry another, ending

the birthright of their daughter.

As a newcomer, a stranger on Cyprus, he owns
no man's loyalty.

—In six months, one ship sent by Cinyras
entered the harbor holding the Greek expedition;

on its deck were fifty-nine clay
ships with fifty-nine clay crews.

Serving on it were Hippolyta's
father and brother.

Cyprians applauded their new King's canny
wit, his sleight-of-hand and boldness; they felt

outrage when Agamemnon, as mere token of
his vengeance, sank the ship, its
crew strapped to its deck . . .

Now before the altar long ago
erected, Hippolyta implores the Furies:—

May the King of the Clay Ships
find the flesh within his bed

clay. Avenge in
torment the dead.

•

As Myrrha is drawn down the dark corridor toward her father

not free not to desire

what draws her forward is neither COMPULSION nor FREEWILL:—

or at least freedom, here *choice*, is not to be
imagined as action upon

preference: no creature is free to choose what
allows it its most powerful, and most secret, release:

I fulfill it, because I contain it—
it prevails, because it is within me—

it is a heavy burden, setting up longing to enter that
realm to which I am called from within . . .

As Myrrha is drawn down the dark corridor toward her father

not free not to choose

she thinks, *To each soul its hour.*

•

Hippolyta carrying a single candle led her through
a moonless night to the bed where
her father waits.

The light disappears.

Myrrha hears in his voice that he is
a little drunk.

She is afraid: she knows that she must not
reveal by gesture or sound
or animal
leap of the spirit that is hers alone, her animal

signature, that what touches him in ways
forbidden a daughter

is his daughter,—

. . . entering his bed, Myrrha must not be
Myrrha, but Pharaoh's daughter come by
law to Pharaoh's bed.

Sweeter than the journey that constantly surprises
is the journey that you will to repeat:—

. . . *the awkward introduction of a foreign object*

which as you prepare to expel
it enters with such insistence

repeatedly that the resistance you have
marshalled against it

failing utterly leaves
open, resistless, naked before it

what if you do NOT *resist it* CANNOT *be reached:—*

you embrace one of the two species of
happiness, the sensation of
surrender, because at the same instant

you embrace the other, the sensation of power:—

. . . *the son whose sister is his mother*
in secrecy is conceived within
the mother whose brother is her son.

Before leaving the bed of sleeping
Cinyras, Myrrha slowly runs her tongue

over the skin of his eyelid.

•

Cinyras insisted to Hippolyta that his
visitor must return a second night, then

a third—

if this new girl proves
beautiful, he will bind her to him . . .

No warrior, Cinyras is a veteran of the combats in
which the combatants think that what they

win or lose is love:—

at the well of Eros, how often he has
slaked the thirst that is but briefly
slaked—;
              he worries that though he still

possesses stamina, an inborn
grace of gesture, the eye of
command, as well as beautiful hands and feet,

thickenings, frayed edges to what he knows was his
once startling
beauty betray how often . . .

The sharp-edged profile still staring from the coins
stamped to celebrate his marriage

mocks him.

And now this creature who
seems when he is exhausted, is un-
renewable,

to make love to his skin,—

. . . who touching its surface seems to
adore its surface so that he
quickens as if he is its surface.

—Myrrha was awakened by the bright lamp
held next to her face. It was held there

steadily, in silence.

The lamp was withdrawn, then
snuffed out.

She heard a sword pulled from its sheath.

Before the sheath clattered to the stone floor
she slipped from the bedclothes.

She heard the sword descend and
descend again, the bedclothes

cut and re-cut.

•

The gods, who know what we want not
why, asked who among them

had placed this thing in Myrrha.

Each god in turn denied it. Cupid
indignantly insisted that his arrows abhorred

anything so dire; Venus seconded her son.

Cupid then said that such
implacable events brought to mind the Furies.

49

The Furies when roused growled that in
a corollary matter they justly again and
again had been beseeched, but upon inspection

exertion by immortals was unneeded.

•

—Sheba's withered
shore . . . Scrub; rocks; deserted coast

facing the sea. Because there is no
landscape that Myrrha's presence does not
offend, she stares at the sea:—

                              across the sea

she fled Cinyras; encircled by the sea
lay the island that she spent childhood
approaching; from Cyprus the sea brought

NOT what she had expected, the King's
minions impelled by the injunction to
shut her, dirt shoved within her mouth, beneath
dirt silenced, exiled forever,—

                              but representatives of
the Queen, informing her of what had
followed her departure:—

                              when Cinyras found Hippolyta
bowing before an altar, he split her with his sword
from the nape to the base of the spine, then after
dragging the body to a parapet overlooking
rocks and sea, with a yell threw it over the edge;—

within hours what
precipitated Myrrha's disappearance was common
gossip;—

within days three warships
appeared in the harbor at Paphos, sent by
Agamemnon, conqueror of Troy.

Word came from them that the people of Paphos could
avoid destruction if, within three days,

Cinyras were delivered to them.

On the third day, as the King's advisors still
debated how to balance honor with prudence,

the King, standing on the parapet from which had
fallen Hippolyta's body,
                              looking out at the ships

leapt. Some said that the cause was
Myrrha; others, Agamemnon.

The eyes of the people of Cyprus
must find offense should Myrrha attempt return . . .

Cyprians are relieved that the Queen, not yet
forty, has decided to accept the unanimous

counsel of her advisors, and remarry.

                    •

—She still smells the whiff of something
fatuous when Cinyras as a matter of

course accepted her adoration.

Now Myrrha teaches her child by daily
telling her child, listening
within her, the story of Myrrha and Cinyras . . .

She failed because she had poured, *tried
to pour*, an ocean into a thimble.

Whatever lodged *want* within her had seen her
vanity and self-intoxication and married

her to their reflection.

The thimble was a thimble—and she had
wronged it . . .

She grew careless because she allowed
herself to imagine that if he once
saw her he must love what he had seen.

Bewildered, betrayed
eyes wait now to accuse her in death.

Her mother once told her:—

*A queen remains a queen only when
what she desires is what she is*

expected to desire.

She would anatomize the world
according to how the world

anatomizes DESIRE. As a girl she had taught

herself to walk through a doorway as if
what she knows is on the other side is
NOT on the other side, as if her father

were a father as other fathers (though
kings) merely are fathers—;
                              will, calculation

and rage replaced in Myrrha what
others embraced as "nature" . . .

Her friends live as if, though what they
desire is entirely what they are
expected to desire, it is they who desire.

Not "entirely"; almost entirely.

—In the final months, when Myrrha again and
again told the child heavier and heavier within her
the story of Myrrha and Cinyras,

she stripped from it words like "ocean" and "thimble."

She was a sentence that he had spoken in
darkness without
knowing that he had spoken it.

She had the memory of taste before she knew
taste itself: *The milk*

that is in all trees. The sweet water that is beneath.

One fruit of all the world's fruit, for
her, tastes—;

she had failed because her fate, like
all fates, was partial.

Myrrha ended each repetition by telling the child
within her that betrayed, bewildered

eyes wait now to accuse her in death.

—Phoenicia; Panchaia; Sheba—

people everywhere lived lives indifferent to the death of
Cinyras—; suffocating, Sheba's
highlands thick with balsam, costmary,
cinnamon, frankincense—;

. . . there is no landscape that her
presence does not offend, so she is free to
prefer this forsaken shore swept by
humid winds, facing the sea.

Her body is dying.

That her body is dying, her labors not yet
finished, her child un-
born, is not what is bitter.

Myrrha addressed the gods:—

*Make me nothing
human: not alive, not dead.*

*Whether I deny what is not in my
power to deny, or by deception*

seize it, I am damned.

*I shall not rest until what has been
lodged in me is neither*

lodged in me,—nor NOT lodged in me.

*Betrayed, bewildered eyes
wait for me in death.*

*You are gods. Release me, somehow, from both
life and death.*

54

The gods granted her request. From her toes roots

sprout; the dirt rises to cover her
feet; her legs of which she never had been
ashamed grow thick and hard; bark like disease
covers, becomes her skin; with terror she
sees that she must
submit, lose her body to an alien
body not chosen, as the source of ecstasy is
not chosen—

        suddenly she is eager to submit: as the change

rises and her blood becomes
sap, her long arms long branches, she cannot bear
the waiting: she bends her face
downward, plunging her face into the rising

tree, her tears new drops glistening everywhere on its surface:—

fixed, annealed within its body
the story of Myrrha and Cinyras:—new
body not alive not dead, story
everywhere and nowhere:—

Aphrodisiac. Embalmers' oil. (Insistence of
sex, faint insistent sweetness of the dead undead.)
Sacred anointment oil: with wine an
anodyne. Precious earth-
fruit, gift fit for the birth and death of

prophets:—no sweet thing without
the trace of what is bitter
within its opposite:—

. . . *MYRRH, sweet-smelling*
bitter resin.

•

Soon the child, imprisoned within the tree,
sought birth. Lucina, Goddess of Child-Birth, helped

the new tree contort, the bark
crack open,—

        . . . pretty as Cupid in

a painting, from the bitter
vessel of Myrrha and Cinyras Adonis was born.

We fill pre-existing forms, and when
we fill them, change them and are changed:—

day after day Myrrha told the child
listening within her her story . . .

Once grown to a man, beautiful as Cupid were
Cupid a man, Myrrha's son

                by his seductive

indifference, tantalizing
refusals tormented love-sick Venus.

Ovid tells us that upon Venus Myrrha's
son avenged his mother.

His final indifference is
hunting (to Venus' horror) the boar

that kills him . . .

Venus did not, perhaps, in her own person
intervene in the fate of Myrrha and Cinyras,—
but children who have watched their parents'
blighted lives blighted in the service of Venus

must punish love itself.

•

O you who looking within the mirror discover in
gratitude how common, how lawful your desire,

before the mirror
anoint your body with myrrh

precious   bitter resin

III

On such a night, at such an hour,

when the inhabitants of the temple of
delight assume for each of us one
profile, different of course for each of us,

but for each of us, single:—

when the present avatar of powers not present though
present through him, different for each of us,

steps to the end of the line of other, earlier
inhabitants of the temple of
delight, different for each of us:—

when the gathering turns for its portrait

and by a sudden trick of alignment and light and
night, all I see

the same, the same, the same, the same, the same—

on such a night,

at such an hour

. . . grace is the dream, half-
dream, half-

light, when you appear and do not answer the question

that I have asked you, but courteously
ask (because you are dead) if you can briefly

borrow, inhabit my body.

When I look I can see my body
away from me, sleeping.

I say *Yes.* Then you enter it

like a shudder as if eager again to know
what it is to move within arms and legs.

I thought, *I know that he will return it.*

I trusted in that none
earlier, none other.

•

I tasted a sweet taste, I found nothing sweeter.
Taste.
My pleasant fragrance has stripped itself to stink.
Taste.
The lust of the sweetness that is bitter I taste.
Taste.
Custom both sweet and bitter is
the intercourse of this flesh.
Taste.

The milk that is in all trees,
the sweet water that is beneath.
Taste.
The knife of cutting is the book of mysteries.
Taste.
Bitterness sweetness, eat that you may eat.
Taste.
I tasted a sweet taste, I found nothing sweeter.
Taste.
These herbs were gathered at full noon, which was night.
Taste.

•

. . . *bodies carrying bodies*, some to bury in
earth what offended earth by breathing, others

become the vessels of the dead, the voice erased
by death now, for a time, unerased.

•

infinite the sounds the poems

seeking to be allowed to S U B M I T,—that this

dust become seed

like those extinguished stars whose fires still give us light

•

This is the end of the second hour of the night.

Note

I have treated sources as instances of the "pre-existing forms" mentioned in the first sentence of "Borges and I"; and done this so freely that it needs acknowledgment. "As the Eye to the Sun" uses as building blocks phrases, sometimes reversed, from George Long's Marcus Aurelius. "Adolescence" is a "found" poem, carved out of anonymously-published prose. "The Return" steals from Michael Grant's translation of *The Annals of Tacitus,* as well as versions by John Jackson, Alfred John Church and William Jackson Brodribb. David Cairns' *The Memoirs of Hector Berlioz* lies behind the first part of "The Second Hour of the Night"; A *Manichaean Psalm-Book,* translated by C. R. C. Allberry, suggested the "taste" litany; the poem throughout is indebted to Stephen MacKenna's translation of Plotinus.

F.B.

DEMCO